The Dakota Image

A Photographic Celebration

The Dakota Image

A Photographic Celebration

Text by Bill Schneider

Published by
Falcon Press Publishing Co., Inc.

Library of Congress Number 80-83707

ISBN 0-934318-02-6

Manufactured in the United States of America

Distribution and Marketing: Falcon Press, P.O. Box 279, Billings, MT 59103
Editorial and Production: Falcon Press, P.O. Box 731, Helena, MT 59601
Text: Bill Schneider
Photo Editor: Michael Sample
Design: Michael Sample and Bill Schneider
Lithography: The Lowell Press
Typesetting: The Helena Letter Shop
Color Separation: Wallace Engraving
Front Cover Photos: Doris Fahlstrom (farmer), Jerry Manley (pheasant),
    Michael Sample (flower), Russ Hanson (sun dogs) and South Dakota
    Division of Tourism (Mount Rushmore).
Back Cover Photo: D.A. Buehler

Prologue:

Something To Celebrate

Of all fifty states, the Dakotas may be the most unknown, unappreciated and yes, uncelebrated.

Far too many Americans place the Dakotas —often interchanging states because they don't realize the difference—at the butt end of their jokes. They may have heard that this is a cultural wasteland, devoid of scenic beauty, where a few hardy souls continually battle wolves and savages to eke out a marginal existence.

Dakotans who have traveled widely and discussed their homeland with others would verify this misconception. During introductions, somebody announces that they hail from Colorado . . . or Montana, Maine, Florida or just about any other state . . . and people politely and routinely respond: "I've always wanted to go there." When somebody announces that they come from North Dakota or South Dakota, the response is strikingly different: "Oh, that's too bad. Don't you like it here?"

Sometimes, it's said in jest, sometimes not. But there's little difference; the barb is still felt.

Perhaps these jesters haven't seen—or even heard of—the Theodore Roosevelt National Memorial Park, Roughlock Falls, the Glacial Lakes, the International Peace Gardens, Devil's Lake, the Needle's Eye, the Turtle Mountains. Nor have they chased Dakota pheasants through a patch of sunflowers or boated on "the Great Lakes," the massive reservoirs on the Missouri River. They could not possibly have viewed the regular procession of postcard sunsets, studied pronghorns or bison grazing a lush prairie swale, filled a stringer with hefty northerns or walleye or relived the Old West amid the numerous historic sites and modern re-enactments.

Critics have undoubtedly heard of Mount Rushmore and the Badlands, but probably don't know which state they're in or whether it's safe to go there.

They have heard of the famed characters of the Wild West—Calamity Jane, Wild Bill Hickok, Sitting Bull, Crazy Horse and others, but rarely relate them with the Dakotas.

A bit extreme? Yes.

But rest assured that the Dakotas have not enjoyed the reputation they deserve.

Tourism agencies and organizations have worked hard to undo long-standing misconceptions about the Dakotas. Hopefully, *The Dakota Image* can add clout to their presentations, for even a quick look at the book confirms that the Dakotas have something to celebrate.

This is America's heartland. Pierce County, North Dakota is, in fact, the geographical center of North America.

The scenery may not include snow-capped peaks, crescendoing alpine streams or palm-studded seashores, but does that mean it lacks scenic qualities? Hardly. Where is it written that the prairie landscape doesn't qualify as scenic?

Quite to the contrary—as this book unequivocally establishes—the Dakotas offer as much scenic grandeur as any state—and more for those who appreciate the elegance, diversity and fertility of the Great Plains.

It's not the instantaneous grabber of a sheer-sided canyon or cloud-brushing mountain. It's a gentle beauty that unfolds subtly until the unsuspecting onlooker suddenly realizes that this may be one of the country's most awe-inspiring landscapes, suitable for any travelogue.

The productive prairie not only supports an agricultural El Dorado, but an abundance of animal and plant life. Wildlife, for instance, is as much a crop as wheat, with the yield reflected by the land's fertility. On this characteristic, the black earth of the Dakotas is rarely surpassed.

Regardless of the diligence of tourism promoters, however, there will always be doubters —those who view the prairie as a boring, treeless intermission between eastern urban areas and the shining mountains of the Rocky Mountain West. They mad dash, lead-foot on the accelerator, down an interstate highway or fly over in pressurized luxury at 30,000 feet reading *The New Yorker*.

But those who must have a mountain in their camera's viewer may happen across the Black Hills of southwestern South Dakota. Here is a vest pocket edition of the Rocky Mountains with the mountains, canyons, forests and streams so often revered by vacationers. Harney Peak, at 7,242 feet, is the highest point east of the Rockies, and the surrounding forestlands have all the ingredients of mountain lore—ski slopes, trout streams, elk and mountain goats, waterfalls, hiking trails, gold mines, ghost towns—to name a few.

Still, this is merely a mountainous outpost in a land generally drawn taut and dry across America's mid-section. The prairie—where the endless sky meets a horizon unbroken by cliffs or conifers—holds the real charm of the Dakotas.

And then there are the people who work that land, the agrarians of the Dakotas, good folks with divergent ancestories—Scandinavian, German-Russian, Dutch, New England and

others. Through history and into modern America, they have maintained a rare toehold in the rapidly disappearing frontier spirit.

Today, as a century ago, a traveler lost in a blizzard can expect, at the sight of any abode, to be taken in, fed and put up for the night, if necessary. Time hasn't wilted this, or many other, Dakota traditions.

Dakotans may be small in number (about nine people per square mile compared with nine-hundred-and-fifty-three per square mile in New Jersey), but they stand tall, full of neighborly instincts and down-home graciousness.

When asked what they miss most about the Dakotas, transplants to other states frequently answer, "the people." Rarely can they explain what exactly it is about the people, just that they miss them. It's just one of those things that has to be experienced, not explained.

Dakotans have grown up with adversity, from the days of the sodbusting and range wars, through the Depression and Dust Bowl and into the tough economics of modern times, enduring an uncooperative climate all the way. They must be strong to cope with—and then live in harmony with—a vast, unpredictable land. They have toiled tirelessly, through the decades, until they actually reflect—physically and mentally—the prairie's vitality and productiveness.

Unlike some states, the ethic of hard-work-pays still thrives here, and unemployment levels routinely rate much lower than the national average.

To really know the Dakotas, one must first know the people.

Although the past most definitely lingers here, progress has not been forsaken. The Dakota economy makes full use of recent technology, and cultural advances haven't gone unnoticed.

Granted, trends often reach the Dakotas months after they preview in New York City. But Dakotans like to take a closer look at change before allowing it. Critics should relish, not ridicule, such scrutiny. A dose of it may make their state a better place.

All in all, the Dakotas are the kind of place that can make anybody feel small—for it's a long way to the horizon.

The Great Plains are appropriately named. Yet, the Dakotas have never won a popularity contest. Maybe, just maybe, *The Dakota Image* can help change this.

The Black Hills are the obvious exception, rising abruptly like a mountainous island from a grass ocean. These mountains are called hills because of their Indian name, *Paha Sapa*. There was no word for mountain in the Indian dialect.

Forever sacred to the Sioux and briefly dominated by the gold-seeker, the Black Hills are now conceded to the recreationist and tourist, for *Paha Sapa* has become a recreational wonderland. It has all the ingredients—by everybody's standards.

Mount Rushmore National Memorial, the Shrine of Democracy, undoubtedly holds the honor as the most famous landmark in the Dakotas. Millions have come to view Gutzon Borglum's creation, the stern faces of George Washington, Abraham Lincoln, Thomas Jefferson and Theodore Roosevelt chipped out of solid granite. It's the largest sculpture undertaken since the time of the ancient Egyptians. It took fourteen years to finish (in 1941), but it will thrill tourists for centuries to come. It symbolizes the greatness and durability of America.

Both North Dakota and South Dakota have large tracts of the ultimate example of the erosive powers of nature, the badlands. Today, the badlands have become a highly sought tourist attraction for both states.

Here, nature has gone uncontrolled in eating away the outer skin of the prairie to expose a panorama of color and clay forms—such a display humankind could never duplicate.

Nature goes all out shedding light on the Dakota landscape—brilliant sunsets, rainbows, northern lights and other special effects.

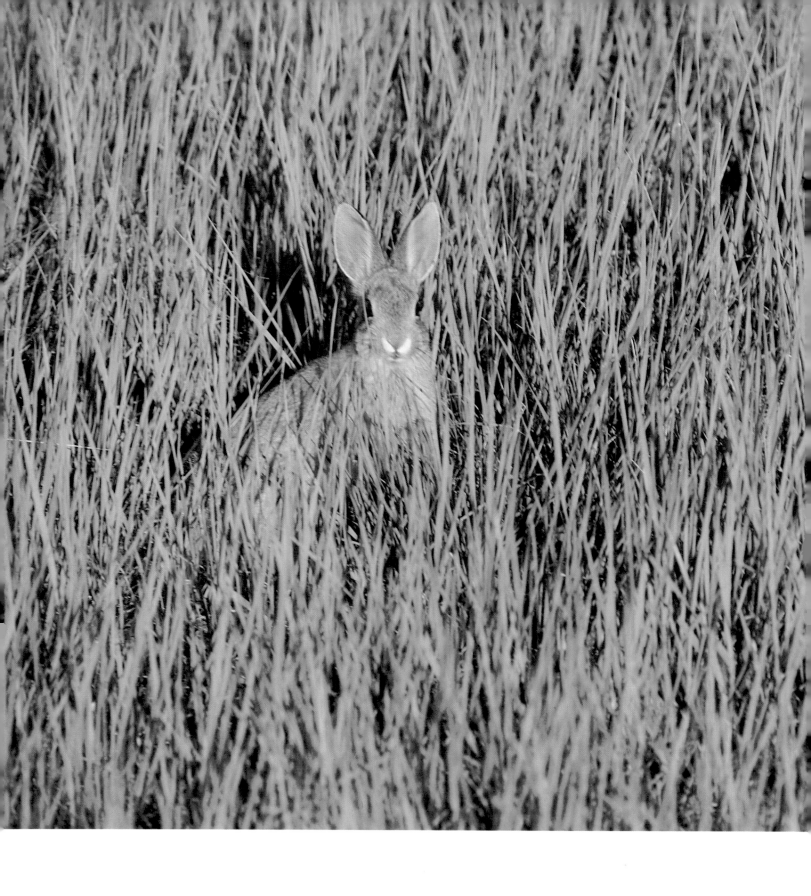

Time has finely honed the instincts and physique of the prairie fauna—the speedy pronghorn, the gregarious prairie dog, the high-jumping jackrabbit and others—to perfectly match their sometimes harsh environment. The prairie can be the land of extremes, so without special adaptation to meet all conditions, the creatures of the grass would have already been evolutionary drop-outs.

Although ideally suited for prairie life, some wild animals weren't equipped to handle the advent of the white man. Thus, the plains grizzly bear and gray wolf have vanished, with others on the brink.

The Dakota grasslands also yield a diverse crop of plant life, including a colorful array of wildflowers. At a distance, the plains can appear uniformly green or brown, but up close, it's alive with color—wild rose, pasqueflowers, prickly pear, coneflowers and many more.

Unusual forms of nature frequent the Dakotas for the enjoyment and bewilderment of those ambitious enough to seek them out. Some stem from the continual battering of the elements; others are the creations of plant and animal artists.

At one time, the Dakotas were almost entirely covered with grass—some tall, some short, depending on the annual precipitation. And most of western and parts of eastern Dakotas still are. The grass clothes the bare land, shields it from the drying wind, softens the beat of the thunderstorm and absorbs the all-important rainfall into the fertile earth.

Once the enormous bison herds were reduced to a mere pittance of their former vastness, domestic stock took over their niche in the great sea of grass. And the Dakotas, particularly the western one-half of both states, became cowboy country. Decade after decade, little changed. The open range was fenced, but roundups, rodeos and branding irons still dominated ranch life. Also surviving, fairly unaltered, was the cowboy, the rough-hewn hero of western lore so prevalent in the child's world of make-believe.

Agriculture heavily dominates the Dakota economy. Since the sod was overturned, the eastern one-half of each state has been a great garden, supplying the rest of the nation—even the world—with corn, oats, rye, barley, flax and of course, wheat, the bread of life. Eastern North Dakota's Red River Valley, to cite one example, has become nationally renowned for its agricultural productiveness—the same affection enshrined by the Corn Palace of Mitchell, South Dakota, complete with exterior decor of locally grown corn.

Modern sport hunters face a stream of threats to their traditional outdoor pursuit—changing societal values that don't always approve of hunting, crowding out of vital wildlife habitat by urbanization, closure of private hunting lands to free public use. But none of these seem as serious in the Dakotas as in many other places.

The Dakotas still offer the hunter an outstanding opportunity. South Dakota, for instance, has long been honored as the Pheasant Capital of the World. And North Dakota is dear to the duck hunter's heart. Large populations of antelope, deer (mule and white-tailed), grouse, turkey, geese, partridge, cottontail, fox, squirrel and a few uncommon species such as bighorn sheep, prairie chickens, elk and bison complete the hunter's paradise.

Hunting has always been a way of life, not just a recreation, in the Dakotas, a trend that promises to continue long into the future.

Although most noted for its warm-water fishing (walleye, northern pike, sauger, largemouth bass, crappie, yellow perch and bluegill), once again the Dakotas provide something different—the ancient dean of fishes, the paddlefish. And trout worshippers need not despair, as the Black Hills have numerous trout-filled lakes and streams.

For all its gentleness and smoothness, the northern Great Plains can be brutal and unforgiving, especially during the frigid winter. Like the prairie grasses and wildlife, the relative newcomers, the Dakota agrarians, have adapted to this land of dramatic seasonal variation.

Epilogue:
Something Worth Saving

Hopefully, the foregoing photographic celebration has helped destroy myths about the Dakotas being a barren hinterland with nothing to see, let alone photograph. That is one reason for *The Dakota Image*.

Such an intention can backfire, though, as too much popularity could ruin it all—crowd out deep-rooted tradition, deface the prairie landscape, discourage rural, hard-working, fun-loving life styles. However, long-time promoters of Dakota tourism see little likelihood of such an overkill.

Perhaps the most oft-used cliche is "a picture is worth a thousand words." Does it follow, then, that a hundred pictures are worth a hundred thousand words? If so, this book may have taught "readers" a lengthy lesson about the Dakotas.

For starters, it may have taught them that some of the Dakotas' most admirable attributes are sparseness of population, abundance of elbow room, shortage of tension-ridden relations and a relatively unpolluted environment—at least when compared to urbanized areas.

These special qualities distinctly separate, and perhaps elevate, the Dakotas from more populous places. They are also the first qualities to disappear under a wave of resource development and population escalation.

This has already happened in so many places —it can happen here, too. Instead of learning from history, Mankind seems intent on repeating it. Thus, it behooves everybody who cherishes the current charm of the Dakotas to reject "inevitable" change—to keep the Dakotas the Dakotas.

It won't be easy, as the winds of change are building to gale-force. The remoteness—even the lowly reputation—of the Dakotas may have been its salvation to date. But no more.

Consider, as an example, the nation's frantic search for energy self-sufficiency. This could drastically disrupt rural communities and disfigure the still untrammeled landscape of western North Dakota and South Dakota. Coal—in this case, lignite—has been termed America's energy "ace-in-the-hole." Not surprisingly, development, including extensive coal gasification facilities and large local influxes of "outside" workers, is well underway in western North Dakota.

Likewise, prospects of large-scale uranium development looms over the Black Hills region. And oil and gas exploration is booming wherever there's potential.

One virtue of the prairie is the ability to recover. It has recovered from past abuse, and it might again.

Then, it might not.

Today's technology makes a much heavier imprint on the land. Breaking sod behind horses hardly compares with twelve-bottom plows and four-wheel-drive tractors, nor does a pick-and-shovel prospector compare with a modern strip miner with seventy-five-yard draglines.

A century ago, developers could sink a hundred-foot shaft or turn over one-hundred-

and-sixty acres. Now, they can level a prairie butte, drain lakes and rivers and cultivate thousands of acres. Can we still rely on the prairie's ability to replenish itself?

Even more serious than the physical threat, however, is the possible demise of Dakota culture. Witness the threat to the family farm posed by hard economic times and corporate farming. What would the Dakotas be like without the family farm? Hard to even imagine.

One thing is certain. The world demand for agricultural products must escalate as population increases. The trend may be delayed by government intervention, but sooner or later, it will affect the Dakotas, hopefully in a positive way.

Perhaps all progress can be accommodated without completely scrambling Dakota society. Perhaps not.

The key word, then, is caution. Dakotans should be ultra-cautious in deliberating the developer's plans, both trivial (but often incremental) and grandiose. The promises of progress don't always come true.

Right now, the Dakotas display a sense of harmony far greater and secure than most

places. Just as the prairie dog and jackrabbit are perfectly evolved to the prairie environment, so now, after a century or so, are the plainsmen, the people of the Dakotas. Their society, their tradition, even their physical appearance are now suited to the land they inhabit, North Dakota and South Dakota. Their environment is, for the most part, still untethered, unknown, unshamed.

It's a gallery of nature's choicest scenes, often naturally lighted to please even the professional photographer. It's a land of distance, of climatic variation, of historical richness, of agricultural abundance, of raw beauty.

It's a land of diversity—and thus, stability; a land of sunshine, remote places and adaptive fauna—large like the bison or small like the flickertail; a land of fertility, small towns, outdoor people, glacial lakes, invisible air and wave upon wave of grass—some cultivated, some not; a land of eroded badlands, cottonwood gullies, slow-moving rivers, massive reservoirs and flat-topped buttes—all crowned with a crest of purest blue.

It's something worth saving. The previous pages prove it.

Photo Credits

Tom Bean: Pages 5, 23 (bottom), 24-25, 32-33, 37 (right), 43, 44-45, 70-71, 72, 80-81, 90-91, 92.

Allen Blank (Bruce Coleman, Inc.): Page 38 (top).

Jim Brandenburg (Bruce Coleman, Inc.): Pages 23 (top), 66, 73.

D. A. Buehler: Pages 9, 20-21, 42, 68.

Jon Cates: Pages 31, 56, 58, 59, 62-63, 72-73.

Harry Engels: Page 39.

Doris Fahlstrom: Pages 15 (top), 47 (bottom left), 52 (top), 52-53, 64 (left).

Russ Hanson: Pages 37 (left), 64 (top), 86 (top).

Paul D. Jones: Page 16 (bottom).

Jerry Manley: Page 1.

Wilford L. Miller: Page 35 (bottom left).

David Muench: Pages 2-3, 6-7, 18, 19, 26, 34, 36, 38, 40-41, 69, 74-75, 76, 76-77, 88.

James Pollock: Page 67 (middle).

Michael Sample: Pages 27 (bottom), 28-29, 29 (bottom), 30, 35 (middle), 62 (middle), 65, 80.

Todd A. Schweiger: Pages 14-15, 49 (top).

South Dakota Conservation Digest: Pages 27 (top) 35 (top and right), 61, 64 (bottom right).

South Dakota Division of Tourism: Pages 8, 10, 11, 12-13, 13, 16 (top), 46, 47 (top and bottom right), 48, 49 (bottom), 52 (middle and bottom), 55, 57 (bottom), 60.

Phil Trieb: Pages 24, 54, 89.

Gary Withey, Pages 17, 22, 50-51, 67 (top).

Gary R. Zahm: Page 29 (top), 57 (top), 67 (bottom), 78-79, 82-83, 86-87.

Zielsdorf Studio: Pages 15 (bottom), 84-85.